WHY WE LOSE

Dennis Peter Barba, Jr., Ph.D.

IdeaBytes Publishing, Inc.

New York, New York

Cleveland, Ohio

IdeaBytes Publishing, Inc.
130 Church Street #356 New York, New York 10007
8535 Tanglewood Square #246 Chagrin Falls, Ohio 44023
Visit our Web Site at www.ideabytespublishing.com

First Printing: April, 2007

30 29 28 27 26 25 24 23 22 21

Library of Congress Cataloging-in-Publication Data is Available

ISBN 0-9715947-1-6

Book cover design by Adam Witwer
Editor: Kimberly Bonvissuto
Printed in China by Palace Press International

Dennis P. Barba, Jr., Ph.D.

To my wife Monica

Dennis P. Barba, Jr., Ph.D.

TABLE OF CONTENTS

Dennis P. Barba, Jr., Ph.D.

Why We Lose®

Introduction

This book is about a particular type of decision-making. It deals with how we make decisions relating to our portfolios and individual investments. One would think such decisions would be made as part of a long-term strategy with a focus on economics and sound business fundamentals. In reality, these decisions are often made as a result of our emotions. This is why we lose!

This will not be a lengthy book for the following reasons:

- It's obvious why we lose. This will become clear in just a few pages.

- The framework for how we win was laid out decades ago, and these principals have not changed. Furthermore, there is no "new economy" nor have the basic fundamentals of business changed.

- Success in the financial markets can only be achieved over the long-term by:

    - Clearly defining your goals.

    - Identifying the return necessary to achieve your goals.

    - Defining your tolerance for risk.

    - Developing, implementing and refining a strategic plan for the management of your assets.

There is an old saying that correlates to managing our investment portfolios: "If you don't know where you are going you are already lost." Many of us don't know where we are let alone have any idea of where we are going.

This book will outline and attempt to explain the underperformance of the typical individual investor, and discuss why this underperformance occurs.

Additionally, this book will outline a framework for strategic thinking designed to help you understand risk and provide a philosophy to use going forward.

If you are serious about managing your assets in an efficient manner, and interested in both understanding and managing the risk associated with investing in the financial markets, keep reading.

Before you continue remember the following quotes:

"The more things change, the more we must embrace the things that never change."

"The future ain't like it used to be."

"Financial unemotional discipline is learned, not inherited."

We will revisit these quotes at the end of this book. Hopefully, by the time you read the above quotes again you will understand "Why We Lose®" and how you can set yourself up to win.

CHAPTER ONE

The Facts
Speak For Themselves

When speaking to others about investing, it's a certainty someone will be quick to point out how well he or she has done investing his or her funds. However, you can bet that whatever your friends, neighbors or colleagues say they have done in the market is being exaggerated by their ego or imagination. Why such a strong statement? First, 20 years of experience dealing with thousands of individual investors. Second, math, which does not lie.

One of the easiest ways to measure individual investor performance is to compare the performance of an investor's mutual fund holdings with the market averages and the average returns of the mutual funds themselves.

Many people assume mutual funds are long-term investment vehicles that the typical investor will hold for a long period of time.

Let's examine some interesting facts regarding investment performance by the average individual investor.

- According to a study conducted by Dalbar Research, between 1984 and the end of 1998, the average stock fund gained 509% or 12.8% per year. Meanwhile, the typical mutual fund investor, whose average holding period was less than three years, earned 186%, or 7.25% per year[1].

- A more recent study conducted by Dalbar Research in 2004 shows that over the past two decades, the typical stock fund investment earned just 3.51% per year. This compares to an average return for the S&P 500 Index of 12.98% during the same time period[2].

We have all seen the advertisements touting active trading programs promising substantial profits. However, the same 2004

---

[1] Mutual Funds Magazine, March 2000
[2] Quantitative Analysis of Investor Behavior Dalbar, Inc., July 2004

Dennis P. Barba, Jr., Ph.D.

Dalbar study found that the average market timer during the past 20 years actually lost an average of -3.29% annually[3].

Terrance Odean's study of investor behavior found that most day traders during the Internet craze actually lost money even as the price of Internet stocks rose, and that their average tenure in day trading lasted approximately six months[4].

Interestingly enough, it appears that very few mutual fund investors actually invest for the long-term. According to Dalbar, for the 20-year period ending 2004, the average equity mutual fund investor held a fund for just 3.3 years before switching, while the average fixed income fund investor held a fund for just 2.6 years before switching [5].

Assuming you or your financial advisor were skillful or lucky enough to choose a winning fund, it's difficult to earn a decade's worth of performance if the security is only held for three years! Investors think long term in theory. However, in reality investors react according to short-term influences dominated by emotions.

Obviously, there have been numerous studies and countless comments regarding the underperformance of individual investors. However, when one examines the performance of money managers and mutual fund managers, there likewise tends to be a significant amount of underperformance, although not nearly as severe as the individual investor.

It's difficult to find studies demonstrating consistent, long-term outperformance of indices that mutual fund managers attempt to beat. There simply does not seem to be a significant statistical relationship between a fund's past performance that can accurately predict future performance. This leads one to believe that it is difficult to predict outperforming mutual funds

---

[3] Quantitative Analysis of Investor Behavior Dalbar, Inc., July 2004
[4] Burton G Malkiel, *A Random Walk Down Wall Street* (New York: W.W. Norton & Company, 2003), p. 98
[5] Quantitative Analysis of Investor Behavior Dalbar, Inc., July 2004

in advance. The ability of fund managers to consistently predict outperforming securities in advance has been debated for decades.

Several studies confirm the difficulty of picking outperforming funds in advance:

- John Bogle authored a report titled "Selecting Equity Mutual Funds" which covered the period between 1974 and 1990. His study concluded that mutual fund winners from the past significantly underperformed the market in the future.

- Burton Malkiel, in the June 1995 issue of The Journal of Finance, presented data that concluded that in the aggregate, mutual funds have underperformed their respective benchmarks both after expenses, and even gross of expenses.

- Burton Malkiel, in his book A Random Walk Down Wall Street, stated that for the 20 years ending December 2001, the average actively managed, large capitalization mutual fund actually underperformed the S&P 500 by nearly two percentage points per year.

The March 2006 edition of Money Magazine showed a chart comparing ten years worth of performance of the average fund manager verses "the market." Money Magazine compared LargeCap, MidCap and SmallCap fund managers against their respective benchmarks for their slice of "the market."

The results were as follows:

Fund Type	Total Return	Percent Beating Benchmark
LargeCap	7.9%	23%
MidCap	11.7%	16%
SmallCap	11.3%	46%

Dennis P. Barba, Jr., Ph.D.

- Ongoing research has demonstrated that only 3% of active managers have been able to beat their respective benchmark over a period of 10 years or more[6] .

Interestingly enough, as I was writing this section of the book, a package arrived in the mail from Credit Suisse Asset Management titled "Credit Suisse Funds Performance and Statistics" for the second quarter of 2005. Credit Suisse Group is one of the world's largest financial organizations. According to this publication, Credit Suisse Asset Management manages approximately $352.2 billion for institutions and individuals worldwide. Credit Suisse has always been a well-known and prestigious financial institution. I was curious to see how well their funds have performed relative to their investment benchmarks. We examined all equity and fixed income funds having at least five years worth of performance. We examined the longest period of time reported in the publication. For example, if they reported a 10-year performance number and the inception date was seventeen years, we used the 17-year number. We included the Common Class, Advisor Class, A shares, B shares and C shares if applicable, and included any sales charge associated with each share class.

In this report there were approximately 17 equity mutual funds. Only two of the 17 funds outperformed their respective investment benchmark. Approximately 88% of these mutual funds underperformed their benchmark index!

In order to be fair, I decided to perform the same analysis with the next two financial institutions sending prospectuses to my home or office. In early 2006, a large envelope arrived from Goldman Sachs Asset Management. In this packet were three prospectuses dated December 29, 2005. The prospectuses were as follows: Goldman Sachs Domestic Equity Funds, Goldman

---

[6] www.indexfundsday.com/pressreleases.aspx

Sachs Structured Equity Funds and Goldman Sachs International Equity Funds. A week later another prospectus arrived: Goldman Sachs Taxable Fixed Income Funds dated February 25, 2005.

Goldman Sachs, founded in 1869 is one of the oldest, largest, and most well respected investment banking firms in the world. Some of the world's brightest financial minds work for Goldman Sachs.

We spent a few hours reviewing the approximately 57 funds included in the Goldman Sachs equity mutual fund prospectuses. Each fund has a stated benchmark against which it is measured. Likewise, within the equity prospectuses there are general summaries of the investment approaches of the various fund managers:

- Proprietary Computer-Optimized, Research-Enhanced Models developed by the Quantitative Equity team

- Momentum theme

- Belief that equity markets are inefficient

- And many more...

There were approximately 57 equity mutual funds within the three Goldman Sachs equity prospectuses. These consisted of A, B and C shares of each respective mutual fund. We examined the returns of each mutual fund before taxes verses the returns of each mutual fund's respective benchmark index since the inception of each fund.

Out of 57 equity mutual funds, only fifteen or 26% outperformed their benchmark index. Approximately 74% of the funds actually underperformed their respective benchmark index. The returns of the Goldman funds after taxes on distributions demonstrate even further underperformance.

The third company to send a prospectus was the WM Group

of Funds. WM Advisors, investment advisor to WM Group of Funds, began as Composite Research & Management Co., which in 1939 launched one of the first 50 mutual funds in the United States. Today WM Advisors is an independently managed subsidiary of Washington Mutual Inc., one of the nation's most prestigious financial services firms. I received a prospectus dated March 1, 2006, for the WM Strategic Asset Management Portfolios. For this group of funds we examined class A and B shares, as all other share classes were recently created. For the Strategic Asset Management Portfolios, WM created a Capital Market Benchmark for each fund. This Capital Market Benchmark is intended to represent a relevant proxy for market and portfolio performance. For example, the Capital Market Benchmark for the WM Conservative Growth Portfolio consists of 80% S&P 500 Index and 20% Lehman Brothers Aggregate Bond Index. There were 10 funds examined within this prospectus. Not one of these mutual funds outperformed their Capital Market Benchmark. 100% of the funds underperformed.

WM included another prospectus dated March 1, 2006, for the WM Group of Funds that included: Equity Funds, Fixed-Income Funds, Municipal Funds and their Money Market Fund. We examined approximately 18 equity funds, of which eight (44%) outperformed their investment benchmarks. This means that approximately 66% of the WM Equity Funds underperformed their respective investment benchmarks.

In fairness to Credit Suisse, Goldman Sachs and WM, it is not possible for an individual investor to invest directly in every benchmark index mentioned in the prospectus. Additionally, the benchmark index performance numbers do not reflect any deduction for fees, expenses or taxes. I should note that we only examined the pre-tax performance numbers of each mutual fund. Had we examined the after-tax returns, the results would have faired much worse for most funds. Finally, you would want to compare the risk of each mutual fund against the risk of each respective benchmark to measure the efficiency of each fund's returns. We will talk more about this later in the book. Even for well-respected institutions like Credit Suise, Goldman Sachs and WM, it is extremely difficult to consistently beat the market over long periods of time.

Underperformance is not limited to equity investors. The results for fixed income fund and money fund investors likewise demonstrate underperformance:

According to Dalbar, the average fixed income investor realized an annual return of 3.75% compared to average returns of 11.16% for a long-term government bond index between 1984 and 2003. Fixed income market timers likewise end up with poor results. The average market timing fixed income mutual fund investor realized an average annual return of -1.85% from 1984 through 2003[7]

We likewise examined the fixed income mutual fund returns from Credit Suisse, Goldman Sachs and WM.

Credit Suisse referenced approximately ten fixed income mutual funds in their report. Only three of the 10, or 30% of the fixed income funds outperformed their respective benchmark. This means 70% of the fixed income funds did not outperform their investment benchmark.

We likewise examined the performance of the fixed income mutual funds in the Goldman Sachs Taxable Fixed Income Funds Prospectus dated February 25, 2005.

If we again include all A, B and C shares within this prospectus there are a total of approximately 20 mutual funds.

Two of the funds, the Enhanced Income Fund and the Ultra-Short Duration Government Fund, were measured against two

---

[7] Quantitative Analysis of Investor Behavior Dalbar, Inc., July 2004

Dennis P. Barba, Jr., Ph.D.

benchmark indices – The Six-Month U.S. Treasury Bill Index and the One-Year U.S. Treasury Note Index. Both of these funds outperformed the six-month benchmark and underperformed the one-year benchmark. Additionally, both funds underperformed the Lehman Brothers Short (1-2) U.S. Government Index. All but three of the other 18 funds underperformed all benchmark indices mentioned in the prospectus. We found that 17 of the 20 mutual funds, or 85%, underperformed their respective benchmark index.

We likewise examined approximately 14 fixed income and municipal funds that were reported in the WM Group of Funds prospectus. 12 of these funds, or nearly 86%, underperformed their respective benchmark.

Hopefully, it is now becoming obvious that the average individual investor has a very difficult time not only beating the market, but even earning a meaningful fraction of what the market returns. Additionally, it has been very difficult for even the professionals to beat the market or their respective benchmark index consistently for extended periods of time.

Dennis P. Barba, Jr., Ph.D.

CHAPTER TWO

Setting Up
Underperformance

There are three primary reasons why we lose. First, most of us are extremely poor financial managers. Chapter One summarized this underperformance.

Second, most Americans are under-savers. It has been estimated that only 34% of adults between the age of 25 and 44 are saving enough to maintain their current standard of living in retirement. We start on the path to losing right after we enter the work force. Unfortunately, this trend usually continues until we reach the age when fear takes over and we feel forced to take corrective action. It is often too late. In fact, it appears that Americans are now actually spending more than we save. This is obviously quite alarming. An article in the February 1, 2006, edition of *The Wall Street Journal* mentions that "Just 17% of households bothered to fund a traditional or Roth IRA for 2004." We are clearly not saving enough to prepare for retirement!

At the beginning of 2006 the savings rate for U.S. households became negative. Additionally, interest payments as a percentage of U.S. disposable income were at an all-time high of approximately 12%. Further increases in interest rates could place increased pressure on the U.S. consumer's ability to save, as even more of our income will be allocated for interest payments and debt repayment. This can become a never-ending spiral and severely inhibit our ability to save for retirement.

We can take this a step further and think about our senior citizen population. It has been estimated that 83% of households with two senior citizens will need additional income to maintain their current standard of living in 10 years. Likewise, it is estimated that 70% of households with two senior citizens will need additional income to maintain their current standard of living in 20 years. This is a result of under-saving and the mismanagement of our portfolios.

Third, we fail to understand that the performance of the

financial markets, and equities in particular, are random. Contrary to what many purported "experts" claim, it is difficult, if not impossible, to "beat the market" over any extended period of time. Nassim Nicholas Taleb, in his book "Fooled By Randomness," refers to the markets as "randomness traps." Taleb states: "The financial markets are by far the most interesting as luck plays a very large role in them. Furthermore, the kind of luck in finance is of the kind that nobody understands but most operators think they understand. In short, there is no get rich quick scheme that actually works. Far too often we mistake our short-term luck in the financial markets for skill and become overconfident. This usually leads to disaster down the road when our luck turns." We once again become dominated by our emotions and make decisions without regard to any strategic directive.

To summarize, the main factors contributing to our "losing" when it comes to our wealth management are as follows:

- Americans are under-savers.

- Americans are poor financial managers.

- Americans are very emotional when it comes to money, and these emotions are one of the main factors leading to the propensity to be poor financial managers.

- The financial markets are random, and due to a fundamental lack of strategy, we are not prepared emotionally to deal with this randomness.

As a result, most of us do not earn acceptable returns on our investment assets and will not be ready for retirement! Remember, our emotions are almost always based on what just happened. When you make financial decisions based on your emotions, you will likely underperform both the market and your financial objectives.

Dennis P. Barba, Jr., Ph.D.

CHAPTER 3

We Are Emotional Beings

Now that we have established the facts of investor underperformance, we should begin to examine in greater detail why we underperform. There is a simple answer to this question. Most of us lack what I like to call "The Scarcest Commodity.®" In investing, as well as in many other aspects of our life, the scarcest commodity is clarity of thought.

What leads us to unclear thinking? The answer is simple – OUR EMOTIONS!

Let's examine how a typical business owner makes the decision to lease a new color copier. Assume that Dan Smith, the owner of ABC Corporation, is in the market for a new color copier. The four-year monthly lease payment on the type of copier he is contemplating is approximately $450 per month.

Dan may analyze this copier decision for over a month. He is likely to get several quotes from different salespeople, analyze the cost of replacing printer cartridges, and even try and negotiate the residual value of the machine at the end of the lease. Hardly an emotional purchase!

Conversely, let's examine how Dan Smith chooses his stocks and mutual funds. Upon arriving home from work the day after signing his copier lease, Dan receives an investment newsletter in his mailbox. In this newsletter the headline reads, "The Sam Walton of Wireless Communication." The bullet points under this bold headline are as follows:

- "Helped turn a $20 million company into a major electronics player with a $3 billion market cap – in just 24 months."

- "Boosted the stock of one of his companies from $14 to an unprecedented split-adjusted $700 per share – returning a profit of 4,900% to his shareholders."

- "Created another company that went from $2 million to $450 million. Share price jumped from under 50 cents to over $12 – a 2,300% gain."

- "Arranged a corporate merger in the mobile communications industry that gave shareholders a quick 182% gain in just 4 weeks. He may end up owning the company!"

- "Has already begun building the new "Wal-Mart" of portable communications – which you and I can still get in on today on the ground floor."

"Own this company now and enjoy the ride for a possible 300% gain within the next 12 to 24 months!"

The above are quotes from the fall 2003 issue of Tech Stock Insights. I have no idea who the people are who put together this publication, and for what you are trying to learn in this book, it doesn't really matter.

It's important to understand what the front page of this newsletter is designed to accomplish. The answer is simple. Such language is designed to stir your emotions and compel you to keep reading. The ultimate goal is to convince you to purchase a particular stock, or to subscribe to a publication. Both will likely be decisions made very quickly, and based solely on your emotions.

If you continue reading the newsletter, your emotions are even more likely to take over. "A select group of savvy individuals recently made what may be the smartest and most profitable investment of their lives – one with the potential to earn them financial independence, comfort, and security for life. They were all astute enough to get in on the ground floor – of a new opportunity that's poised to return a profit of over 300% within the next 12 to 24 months." Of course, nothing is guaranteed. But the odds – as you'll see – have been unfairly tipped on their side. And the initial investment – which starts at approximately three dollars and fifty cents – is something anyone can afford."

The author then mentions several stocks and states that if you were savvy enough to get in on the ground floor that you would be financially independent. The stocks mentioned were Qualcom, which had a gain of 2,438%: Intel, which had a gain of 4,300%: Cisco, which had a gain of 17,625%: and JDS Uniphase, which had a gain of 930%.

The author was careful to point out "that many of these stocks have taken a beating during the most recent bear market. But over the long term, that doesn't matter. A few savvy investors – those who were able to get in on the ground floor of the "big thing" of their day – made small fortunes from owning these companies."

Nonsense! In reality, it certainly matters that theses stocks have taken a beating. Most of us are not capable of purchasing the best performing stocks and mutual funds at their lows, and knowing exactly — or even approximately, when to get out.

After reading the rest of the newsletter, Dan decides this stock is a "good idea." As a result of this ten-minute analysis on the investment merits of a stock touted in an investment newsletter, Dan decides to purchase 5,000 shares. What were the factors that influenced this decision? Arguably, there was not a compelling reason for this purchase other than a "gut feeling." This type of decision is not much different than choosing fish over chicken for dinner. You sit down at a restaurant, look at the menu, have a feeling "the fish is good here," and choose the fish. Dan spends months vacillating over the decision to lease a copier, and then during the course of ten minutes drops over $15,000 on an impulsive stock purchase. In fact, one could argue that this decision is based on pure greed.

Let's review more specifically what's wrong with the statements in this type of publication:

It's certainly true that a small group of investors were fortunate enough to get in on the above-mentioned investments very early in their history and make tremendous sums of money. What about the average investor? What if you got in at the wrong time?

Let's take a moment and examine the performance of two of these stocks, Qualcom & JDS Uniphase.

First, let's assume you were one of the very few fortunate enough to purchase each of these stocks in their early days and have the savvy to unload your position at or near their highs.

QCOM - Purchase 5,000 shares in 1996 at $5.50 per share. Initial investment $27,500.

QCOM - Sold 5,000 shares in 2000 at $200 per share. Proceeds: $1 million.

This would represent a gain of approximately 3,500%.

JDSU - Purchased 5,000 shares in 1996 at $2.50 per share. Initial investment $12,500.

JDSU - Sold 5,000 shares in 2000 at $153 per share. Proceeds: $765,000.

This would represent a gain of approximately 6,000%.

Both trades would have represented almost unthinkable success for anyone lucky enough to experience this sort of timing.

Let's also examine an investor who purchased shares in 2000 and still held them in 2004:

QCOM - Purchased 5,000 shares in 2000 at $150 per share. Initial investment: $750,000.

QCOM - Sold 5,000 shares in 2004 at $64 per share. Proceeds: $320,000.

This would represent a loss of approximately 57%.

JDSU - Purchased 5,000 shares in 2000 at $100 per share. Initial investment: $500,000.

JDSU - Sold 5,000 shares in 2004 at $4.50 per share. Proceeds: $ 22,500.

This would represent a loss of approximately 96%!

Those unfortunate enough to buy these stocks at or near their highs had much of their net worth evaporate during the 2000-2002 declines.

Even if you were fortunate enough to purchase companies like Qualcom or JDS Uniphase early in the game, one of two things would have likely happened:

First, you would have been unwilling to liquidate the position because you were unwilling to pay the capital gains taxes. Additionally, many of us were convinced that these issues would keep moving higher. After all, the top brokerage analysts were continuing to write glowing reports on these companies, so why would we think anything bad would occur?

Second, you may have become overconfident and actually believed that you were making these enormous paper profits as a result of your skill rather than luck. This became very dangerous. Many investors became so overconfident and greedy that they borrowed against their large gains in the form of margin loans from their brokerage firms. They took this newly created cash and purchased shares of other high-tech or Internet companies, looking to parlay their winnings even further.

The effects for many were life changing. When the markets turned, their large paper profits were wiped out. In many cases much if not all of their original investment was lost. In some instances, investors were left owing the brokerage firms money. Think of the following example:

John Smith takes his $150,000 life savings and buys three technology stocks in the late 1990s. By 2000, the value of his holdings are worth over $2 million. John then begins to borrow money from his broker accumulating margin debt of $1 million.

John now owns $3 million worth of stock positions but he owes $1 million to his brokerage firm in the form of a margin loan against the stocks purchased.

The markets turn and John, unwilling to liquidate his positions and admit defeat, holds on until the very end. What happens?

Let's assume the market value of John's holdings dropped 85%:

John's equity holdings at peak value
$3 million

Margin loan to brokerage firm
($1 million)

Net equity in John's brokerage account
$2 million

Market drops 85%

John's equity holdings at bottom
$ 450,000

John's margin loan to brokerage firm
($1 million)

Net equity in John's brokerage account
($ 550,000)

In this example, John has lost all of his paper gains and his original investment. He actually lost more money than he originally started with.

Fortunately, John's brokerage firm would have placed "margin calls" on his account, forcing him to deposit additional cash or sell securities as the market dropped. So his actual end value may not have been ($550,000). However, this simple example should help you get the picture of the pitfalls involved in assuming excessive risk.

Think of the following statement:

"Investment return is far more dependent on investor behavior than on mutual fund or security performance."

As already mentioned, it's typical for investors to purchase securities based on emotional decisions. We have all read about the great 10-year performance of a mutual fund or money manager. We may have even owned such a fund. I have met people who actually believe the performance numbers reported in prospectuses and the media are merely a fabrication, designed to compel people to send in money. Their rationale for such a statement stems from their experience owning a mutual fund, and not earning the performance stated in an advertisement that compelled their purchase. There are reasons why most mutual fund investors fail to earn the average return of their holdings:

- Mutual fund performance numbers assume an investor made a lump sum investment and actually held the fund for the entire period being reported. Virtually no investors do this.

- The average holding period of an equity mutual fund investor during the 20-year period ending 2003 was just 3.3 years[8].

- As stocks rise, investors pour cash into equity mutual funds.

---

[8] Quantitative Analysis of Investor Behavior Dalbar, Inc., July 2004

Dennis P. Barba, Jr., Ph.D.

- As stocks decline, cash rapidly flows out of equity funds.

- Investors continue to be dominated by emotional investment decisions.

It's common for individual investors to only buy mutual funds that are highly rated by Morningstar. I have always found it quite comical when an investor asks "how many stars does the fund have?" or "I would rather buy fund XYZ because it is a five-star rated fund." What most investors fail to realize is that the "Morningstar system, developed in 1984, was created to provide a practical, simple-to-understand rating that investors could use as a FIRST STEP in making investment decisions.

The star system was not meant to be prescriptive in that it wasn't designed to predict future fund performance."[9]

When an investor makes an emotional decision to purchase a mutual fund based solely on a Morningstar ranking, they are subjecting their investment performance to chance or luck.

There are three types of emotions that make it difficult for us to maintain Clarity of Thought®. These emotions are:

- Fear

- Greed

- Overconfidence

We **Fear** that we will miss out on the potential returns a good investment will provide. After we own an investment for a period of time and the short-run returns are not what we had hoped, we quickly sell the investment and purchase something else that "sounds good." This helps explain why in the 1990s an average of $91 billion of new cash flowed into mutual funds after their best performing quarters.

---

[9] Charles M. Williams, Markus Mullarkey , Andre f. Perold

We fear missing out on a good opportunity, we are fearful of taking losses and we are fearful of missing out on market advances.

We are **Greedy**! It is our greed that prohibits us from selling an investment that no longer exhibits the sound fundamental qualities possessed at the time of purchase. We want to squeeze out every last bit of profit. Likewise, it is our greed that compels us to purchase a $4 stock we believe is going to go to $400, as well as purchase the $400 stock that is on its way to $4.

We are always caught in the middle of the horse race between fear and greed. Fear and greed steal our money and lead to unclear thinking! As a result, it's the "along-the-way" that steers us into trouble during the long journey. Building wealth through the financial markets is a process that takes time. It is not unlike building a successful business. Successful businesses are not built overnight. Conversely, a successful business usually takes decades to build. It is extremely rare to find an entrepreneur who starts a business and sells it for millions within the first few years.

Let's go back to how individual investors buy mutual funds. We already mentioned the flaw in investors' insistence on buying highly-ranked Morningstar funds. Investors believe this is a predictive system. What about the media? When an individual reads a financial publication, or watches a financial show, the recent top performing funds are advertised. It is only human nature to want to own these funds. However, making the decision to purchase a fund solely based on its recent performance is usually a decision based on fear or greed — the fear of not keeping up or missing out on an opportunity, or the greed involved in thinking that one would make a lot of money with the fund. Finally, we hate to see our friends and acquaintances do well. It has been said that there is nothing worse than watching a friend get rich. This greed creates the urge to speculate.

Dennis P. Barba, Jr., Ph.D.

Why is it that mutual fund companies advertise in financial publications? There are very strong economic reasons for mutual fund advertising. The publications have sales people who call on the fund companies. CNBC is in business to generate revenue and make a profit. This cannot be accomplished without advertisers paying to influence our emotions. Additionally, mutual funds advertise to attract money from investors. This is best accomplished by advertising superior past performance in order to compel investors to react emotionally, by purchasing shares of the advertised mutual fund. Who in their right mind would advertise an underperforming mutual fund? A study published in the April 2000 edition of _The Journal of Finance_ analyzed 294 mutual funds advertised in Barron's and Money Magazine. In this study, Prem C. Jain and Joanna Shuang concluded that although most mutual funds pitch their superior performance in the period preceding the advertisement, there is no evidence of superior performance of these same mutual funds following the advertisement. Their results revealed that any past superior performance of advertised mutual funds was not associated with the future results of those same funds. In fact, they found that in the post-advertisement period, the funds, on average, underperform significantly in comparison to the S&P 500.

The pattern continues...Investor reads advertisement... Advertisement shows mutual fund with recent superior performance...Investor becomes greedy and emotional...Investor makes impulsive decision and buys the fund...Investor does not earn advertised returns...Investor sells mutual fund and buys another based on the same types of emotions...Investor repeats behavior for many years...Investor loses!

The third emotion that just kills us is **Overconfidence**. God forbid we have some luck with our early investment choices. Once we choose our first loser, we are so overconfident that we fail to believe we made a bad choice. Many of us suffer from what's known as the ***disposition effect***, which is the human tendency to hold onto our losing stocks while selling our winners. There are many reasons why individual investors continuously hold on to their losing positions:

- The belief that a loss is not realized until the stock is actually sold.

- Failure to tell your spouse, friend or colleague that you made a bad decision and realized a loss.

- Coming to grips with the fact that you were incorrect in your initial emotional judgments…Your initial gut feeling was way off!

The emotions of fear, greed and overconfidence steal our money and lead to unclear thinking. These emotions box us into a corner, leading to a lifetime of underperformance. The example of John margining his JDSU position is a perfect example of fear, greed and overconfidence leading to failure.

Unfortunately, choosing investments based on emotions is not limited to individual investors. Many investment advisors chose investments for their clients in much the same fashion. The following is a typical example:

John Advisor arrives at the office on Monday morning to find a weekly research packet prepared by his firm. While skimming through this report, he comes across a one-page synopsis on a stock, ABC, Inc. After reading 10 bullet points on why the analyst feels this stock will go from 20 to 30, John Advisor decides that ABC is a "good idea." As a result, John Advisor purchases more than 100,000 shares of ABC for more than 100 of his clients, who range in age between 25 and 80.

What's wrong with this scenario? First, the decision to purchase ABC was an emotional decision largely based on a gut feeling. Second, it is doubtful that any significant analysis was contemplated regarding the effects of placing ABC into each of John's client portfolios. Did John analyze if purchasing ABC added risk or diversified risk away from each portfolio? Did John review each client's strategic plan to determine if ABC is appropriate based on the client's risk tolerance, investment objectives and asset allocation strategy? The answer to all is probably no.

When a typical emotional individual investor interacts with an emotional financial advisor, they are entering into a flawed relationship from the start.

Dennis P. Barba, Jr., Ph.D.

CHAPTER 4

Beware of Dynamite!

Hopefully it's now clear that most of us make investment decisions based largely on our emotions. I am going to borrow a quote from Joel Greenblatt in his book "The Little Book That Beats The Market." Joel's quote is among my favorites and, unfortunately, does a good job of describing the typical individual investor.

"Choosing individual stocks without any idea of what you're looking for is like running through a dynamite factory with a burning match. You may live, but you're still an idiot."[10]

Once again we return to John and his JDSU experience. In this case, John not only walked into the dynamite factory holding a burning match, but he was also carrying an open container of paint thinner! Unfortunately for John he sneezed, dropped the match in the open can of paint thinner and "blew himself up!"

Even when creating a portfolio consisting solely of mutual funds, it's not recommended to enter "the dynamite factory." It is far less likely you will "blow yourself up" while playing the "mutual fund shuffle game" in the dynamite factory. However, you are still likely to end up in the burn unit for several months as a result! As I will layout later in this book, Strategy is dynamite's Kryptonite.

Why is it we have such a difficult time allowing strategy to enter into our investment decisions, as opposed to just following our emotions? Why do we seem to enjoy the dynamite factory adventure? I believe much of it stems from our lack of understanding that the capital markets are:

- Efficient

- Random and unpredictable

- Volatile and risky

---

[10] Greenblat, Joel, *The Little Book That Beats The Market.* (New Jersey: John Wiley & Sons, Inc., 2006), p. 100.

Dennis P. Barba, Jr., Ph.D.

Also:

- Investors fail to remain focused.

- Investors fail to execute a long-term strategy.

- Investors fail to control their emotions.

- Investors overweight their recent memories.

- Investors fail to understand the risk inherent in the financial markets.

Again, it's the "along the way" that leads us into trouble during the long journey of building wealth. We are able to think and act strategically when we are engaging in such activates as: purchasing a business, selecting a child's college, researching and selecting a course of treatment for a serious illness, and working through a family crisis. Why do we act so irrational when investing our hard-earned cash?

Dennis P. Barba, Jr., Ph.D.

CHAPTER 5

Efficiency and the Financial Markets

The financial markets are **Efficient**. This is a statement that has been, and will continue to be, the subject of much debate.

Many investment advisors have purported to detect recurring patterns in the movement of common stock prices. These advisors sell their investment information to investors. Many times these advisors market their ability to find inefficiencies in the market. However, many in academia believe this outperformance is more attributable to luck as opposed to skill. They point to the investment advisor's inability to consistently outperform over long periods of time. For the very few who seem to beat the markets or their respective benchmarks, believers in the efficiency of markets say these violations - or anomalies - of the markets are freak, isolated instances that are not applicable to the vast majority of market participants.

The Efficient Market Hypothesis is an idea partly developed in the 1960s by Eugene Fama. It states that it is difficult to beat the market because prices already incorporate and reflect all relevant information. As prices only respond to available information and because all market participants are privy to the same information, no one will have the ability to consistently "out-profit" anyone else. In efficient markets, prices become random, so no investment pattern can be discerned. It is argued that a planned approach to market outperformance cannot be successful. Under the Efficient Market Hypothesis, any time you buy and sell securities you're engaging in a game of chance, not skill. If markets are efficient and current, it means that prices always reflect all information, so there's no way you'll ever be able to buy a stock at a bargain price.

This is also a highly controversial and often disputed theory. Supporters of this model believe it is pointless to search for undervalued stocks or to try and predict trends in the market through any technique (fundamental or technical analysis). This theory has been met with significant opposition, especially from the technical analysts and a new group of economists focusing on what is known as behavioral finance. The technical analysts' argument against the efficient market hypothesis is that many investors base their expectations on past prices, past earnings, back-testing, track records, and other indicators. Since stock prices are largely based on investor expectation, many believe it only makes sense to believe that past prices do influence future prices. Behavioral finance deals with the emotional and behavioral tendencies of individual investors, which we have already discussed in detail. Believers in behavioral finance point to instances when there are anomalies to the market being efficient such as:

- Irrational trades being correlated with each other

- Market inattention

- Individual investor overconfidence

- Individual investors only recognize and consider recent events

- Most individual investors believe they are above average

I personally have strong feelings regarding market efficiency/ inefficiency. First, I believe that in efficient markets, supply and demand dictate market prices. In our financial markets, the availability of information and the technology that makes trade executions almost immediate helps lead to efficient markets.

Even the believers in behavioral finance suggest not betting the whole house on a single strategy or a small group of stocks. They suggest diversifying across a set of strategies. They state that some of these strategies will stop working because the historical back testing could have been due to chance. More importantly, even the behavioral finance camp acknowledges that once an investment strategy that beats the market becomes well known, it may erase the advantage. This supports the efficiency of the markets.

It can be argued that a "bubble" is a sign of an inefficient market. I do not agree. There are certainly instances when demand is far greater than supply in a market. When this occurs, prices usually rise. This is a basic principle of economics. Part of what helps make financial markets efficient is that during periods of "irrational exuberance" or excess speculative demand by emotional investors, the market will provide such opportunities. If the financial markets know in advance that excess speculation will create asset price bubbles, the markets could arguably function less efficiently.

Financial or asset class bubbles have existed in global financial markets almost as far back as one can research.

- The tulip-bulb speculative craze in the 1500s in Holland.

- Metallic coins during the Holy Roman Empire during the 1600s.

- The South Sea bubble in the 1700s when people speculated in England over future trade to the South Seas.

- Import commodities and Banks in Europe during the 1700s and 1800s.

- Railroad stocks in the U.S. during the 1800s.

- Stock market speculation and subsequent crash in the 1920s.

- The new issue speculation during the 1960s.

- Biotech stock speculation in the 1980s.

- Japanese real estate speculative bubble of the twentieth century. According to Burton Malkiel in his book "A

Random Walk Down Wall Street, *"by 1990, the total value of all Japanese property was estimated at nearly $20 trillion – equal to more than 20% of the entire world's wealth and about double the total value of the world's stock markets. America is 25 times bigger than Japan, in terms of physical acreage, and yet Japan's property in 1990 was appraised to be worth five times as much as all American property. Theoretically, the Japanese could have bought all the property in America by selling off metropolitan Tokyo. Just selling the Imperial Palace and its grounds at their appraised value would have raised the cash to buy all of California."*[11]

During the bull market of the late 1990s there were many instances when demand outstripped supply. Investor interest in new technology and Internet IPOs rose by the week. Did it make sense for a newly issued company with little or no sales to become a billion-dollar market cap stock within two days of going public? Probably not, but how is this inefficient? Supply and demand dictates the trading price of each security.

It is through an efficient market that supply and demand set the price.

The bear market of the early 2000s was, in my opinion, an efficient market bringing prices back to reality. This is a classic case of investors believing the market is inefficient and having confidence that "beating the market" can be easily accomplished. In fact, it has been argued that in order for a market to truly become efficient, there must be a group who perceives that the market is inefficient and possible to beat.

With every past price bubble, the market has found a way to correct the price imbalance. Sometimes this can be a slow and painful process, depending on how much emotional demand

---

[11] Malkiel Burton G., *A Random Walk Down Wall Street.* (W.W. Norton & Company, 2003), p. 77.

drives up and then consequentially, drives down prices.

Technical and fundamental analysts can use changes in supply and demand to take advantage of what they feel is an overvalued or undervalued security. However, this does not mean that the markets are inefficient. Many will argue that the analyst was simply lucky for a period of time. Furthermore, let's assume a professional discovered a technique that back-tested or data mined beat the market. Typically, as soon as this data is made available to the market, the advantage disappears. The magazine _Institutional Investor_ stated in 1993 that "The proliferation of computers and databases has made it harder for everybody – analysts, portfolio managers and amateurs alike – to make money the old-fashioned way, by finding stocks whose value is not yet recognized by the market."[12]

Finally, as I write this book there is much talk regarding the speculative bubble in real estate prices in the United States.

No one is certain which areas of the country will experience housing price declines or when. However, it appears that the increases in Florida real estate will have a difficult time continuing annualized appreciation rates of 15% to 20%. According to Richard DeKaser, senior vice president and chief economist of National City, approximately 38% of the U.S. housing market is at an extreme overvaluation level. According to National City, Naples, Florida is 84% overvalued by their models.[13]

An interesting quote from an April 1890 Chicago Tribune editorial will likely shed some light on what happens during speculative manias, including the recent speculation in U.S. real estate: "In the ruin of all collapsed boons is to be found the work of men who bought property at prices they knew perfectly well

---

[12] Debbie Galant, "Why Quants Need Stock Pickers", Institutional Investor, November 1, 1993)

[13] Barrons. February 13, 2006. Page 27.

Dennis P. Barba, Jr., Ph.D.

were fictitious, but who were willing to pay such prices simply because they knew that some still greater fool could be depended on to take the property off their hands and leave them with a profit." [14]

The Efficient Market Hypothesis does not dismiss the possibility of anomalies in the market that result in the generation of excess profits. In fact, market efficiency does not require prices to be equal to fair value all of the time.

Prices may be over or undervalued only in random occurrences, so they eventually resort back to their mean value.

Followers of Fama and the Efficient Market Hypothesis argue that investors who outperform the market do so not out of investment skill, but by luck. With such a large number of investors, the laws of probability will yield a number who outperform the market. What you are likely to discover during any research into investment performance, is that a very small percentage of individual investors have outperformed the market indices consistently over time. Likewise, a very small percentage of professional money managers consistently outperform the benchmark indices over time. This is consistent with the Efficient Market Hypothesis. Furthermore, in the rare instances that a fund or manager has been able to outperform the market for any period of time, it has been accomplished by assuming substantially more risk. It can be argued that this fact, likewise, points to the efficiency of the market.

Again, when one reviews the long-term returns of most professional money managers and mutual fund managers, it becomes apparent that the overwhelming majority do not outperform the S&P 500 Index, the Dow Jones Industrial Average or even their stated investment benchmark. Furthermore,

---

[14] *Charles P. Kindleberger, Manias, Panics, and Crashes A History of Financial Crises.* Fourth Edition. (John Wiley & Sons 2000), p.111.

as discussed in the beginning of this book, individual investors earn only a fraction of what the market returns.

Another interesting observation regarding the reporting and advertising of the outperformance of professional money managers, is the relative absence of information regarding those who fail and exit the business. Quite simply, we only hear about the winners. Who advertises their underperformance or the fact that they are going out of business? Taleb states, "We only see the winners. That it is natural for those who fail to vanish completely. Accordingly, we only see the survivors. By only seeing the survivors, we end up with a mistaken perception of the odds of success."[15]

An article in the July 2006 issue of _Entrepreneur Magazine_ further substantiates Taleb's observation. _Entrepreneur_ published a concept known as "survivorship bias." Survivorship bias has to do with the fact that 900 to 1,200 mutual funds cease to exist each year. "As a result, when investors measure the past performance of a group of funds against a benchmark, the funds look like they performed better than they actually did because the worst performers are not included."[16] _Entrepreneur_ also reported: "Savant Capital Management found that this survivorship bias caused Morningstar's published data to incur inflated returns in 41 of its 42 categories by an average of 1.6% per year between 1995 and 2004."[17]

Michael J. Mauboussin mentions a study by John Bogle of Vanguard. Bogle's study found study that 50% of mutual funds failed in the 1990s, and almost 1,000 failed in 2000 through 2004 alone."[18]

It is not important for you to believe that the financial markets

---

[15] Nassim Nichols, Fooled By Randomness The Hidden role of Chance in Life and in the Markets. Second Edition. (Thomson Texere 2004), p. 127.

[16] Entrepreneur. July, 2006. p. 66

[17] Entrepreneur. July, 2006. p. 66

[18] Michael J. Mauboussin. More Than You Know Finding Financial Wisdom in Unconventional Places. New York. (Columbia University Press. 2006), p 20.

are completely efficient all of the time. There will likely continue to be inefficiencies that provide quick windows of opportunity for professionals. Likewise, there will always be those who find ways to outperform for a period of time.

Additionally, as the number of people participating in the market increases, the laws of math will lead to a greater likelihood of a higher number outperforming the markets. Will this outperformance be due to skill or random luck? This is a question that will likely never be answered with complete certainty. However, it is critical for individual investors to understand that the markets are generally efficient.

If you are an investor who believes in the efficiency of the capital markets, then you should believe in the following:

1. The markets are efficient.

2. The markets self correct.

3. The average will play its role as long as you start with the right mix, and allow yourself to stay in the game.

Dennis P. Barba, Jr., Ph.D.

CHAPTER 6

The Randomness and Unpredictability of the Financial Markets

In the previous chapter we discussed the concept of market efficiency. If we believe the financial markets are largely efficient then we will use six basic assumptions going forward:

1. The financial markets are generally efficient as they relate to the typical individual investor.

2. Most relevant information is priced into the markets.

3. Any new information or "secret investment strategies" once known are quickly assimilated and priced into the market. Furthermore, once the purported advantage of a "secret investment strategy" becomes published and available to the investing public, the advantage quickly dissipates.

4. It is not possible to consistently predict how the markets, mutual funds or individual money managers will perform. Likewise, it is not possible to consistently predict which funds, stocks or money managers will outperform the market or their investment benchmark.

5. Randomness or luck plays a role in who outperforms the markets and by how wide a margin. It is generally understood that it's difficult for individuals and the vast majority of professionals to beat the market over extended periods of time.

6. We accept the fact that the outcomes in the financial markets are random. Additionally, we accept that in the absence of strategy, our investment returns will be random and largely based on luck.

If we believe the markets are efficient, then we must believe in the concept of randomness. If the returns of the financial markets are not predictable then they are in fact, random. Over time, no one has been able to consistently discover recurring patterns that guarantee investment success. We introduced the term "Randomness Traps" earlier in the book. If you believe in the efficiency of markets then it only makes sense that price movements can and do move in unpredictable and random ways.

What exactly is randomness? According to the dictionary, the word random is used to express apparent lack of purpose, cause or order. The term randomness is often used synonymously with a number of measurable statistical properties, such as lack of bias or correlation. Ironically, this sounds similar to how many of us invest our money. We seem to lack purpose, cause or order. Relying on our emotions when making investment decisions, will lead to a greater dependence on randomness in achieving success.

It is our unwillingness to accept randomness that causes us to make emotional-based investment decisions. It's difficult for individual investors to believe in randomness, as the financial markets are "**Noisy.**" There is a consistent and ever-increasing amount of "**noise**" or "**junk**" surrounding the financial markets. What is the primary purpose of the financial media? The answer to this question can be debated indefinitely. One simple economic explanation is that the media exists to sell advertising to generate profit as a business entity. As a result, the media must create emotional reactions to compel us to watch their television shows or read their publications. Earlier we mentioned the tendency of mutual funds to advertise their outperformance, and the lack of correlation of future fund returns, as they relate to their advertised performance.

With so many "experts" being interviewed, articles being written and advertisements touting consistent outperformance, it can be difficult for the average person to believe that future outcomes are not already known.

Fifteen years ago the only way for an individual investor

to receive information on stocks, mutual funds and money managers was through someone affiliated with Wall Street. This is no longer the case, as information is now available almost instantaneously to all investors. Does this make for more efficient markets? Arguably yes, as everyone can have access to, disseminate and price this information into the markets.

However, I believe this instantaneous availability of information leads to greater confusion for investors. Pay close attention to the media and you will begin to notice that about half of the "experts" seem to be arguing why the markets will move higher, and the other half seem to be predicting the end of the world. All of this noise helps lead us toward emotional, non-strategic investment decisions.

In summary, the instantaneous availability of noise leads to confusion, which leads to more emotions, which leads to investment decisions dominated by emotions. Regardless of how much you read and watch television, the fact will remain that what happens next in the markets will continue to be random. Spending 20 hours per week studying the opinions of the "experts" is not going to remove randomness from your portfolio, and will likely not do much in the way of helping you control your emotions.

An investor can do their research by watching financial shows and reading financial publications, and still make money in the market only due to randomness. Likewise, we can complete all of our research and still lose money over the short-term due to randomness.

This new and instantaneous availability of information now allows us to check our portfolio holdings as often as we like. Some investors check their accounts several times during the course of each business day. The odds of any portfolio making money over a shorter period of time such as a day, week or month are more subject to randomness than a portfolio increasing in value over longer periods of time such as a quarter, year or five-year period.

Think about how we managed our 401(k) accounts 15 years ago. Once a quarter we received a statement with a breakdown of our holdings and possibly a comparison of the current value with the previous quarter. If our account dropped in value during the quarter we might have felt emotional and thought about making a change in our portfolio. However, we were unable to log onto our computers and make an emotional change within minutes. We had to locate the toll-free number, wait on hold, and then spend 30 minutes discussing how to make a change with a person on the other end of the phone. Compare this to our near instantaneous ability to view our portfolios by the minute. It is now possible to have your home page on your computer display your portfolio holdings. We can literally view the changes in our portfolio dozens of times during any single day and hundreds of times during the course of any given month. The influences of randomness over very short periods of time are more pronounced. As a result, it has become increasingly easier to make emotional investment decisions.

It should now be obvious that randomness leads to an increase in emotional investing. It is common for most of us to mistake our luck for skill. This mistake likewise leads to an increase in emotional decisions. Remember, we are always influenced by what happened most recently. If our recent experience in the markets was positive, our emotions will cause us to become overconfident and aggressive. Likewise, should our recent experience result in sharp losses, emotions will once again dominate. Either we will "throw in the towel" and liquidate our portfolio or we will become even more aggressive in an effort to recoup those losses.

This quote by Taleb applies perfectly to those who mistake

their luck for skill: "You can mispredict everything for all of your life yet think you will get it right next time." [19] Our unwillingness to understand the power of randomness and accept its dangers is one of the first steps toward walking into the "dynamite factory." It is important to understand that random events are not expected. In many aspects of our life it's the unexpected that causes us the most frustration.

I would like to introduce a concept that I call "The Efficiency of Randomness." This is a simple concept and should be a fundamental belief as you invest your money. The Efficiency of Randomness accepts that the financial markets are random, and understands the occurrence of random events and the consequences of randomness. The consequence of randomness means that every so often you or your financial advisor will be wrong. It's OK to be wrong! The objective of investing is not to be correct all of the time. The key is to survive over the long-term and not let your emotions cause you to give up. Accepting the Efficiency of Randomness means you have to accept the fact that being wrong and losing money is completely expected and normal.

When you are dealing with unknown future results, how can you expect anything other than being wrong on occasion?

---

[19] Taleb Nassim Nichols, Fooled By Randomness The Hidden role of Chance in Life and in the Markets. Second Edition. (Thomson Texere 2004), p. XXI.

Dennis P. Barba, Jr., Ph.D.

CHAPTER 7

The Financial Markets Are Risky!

If randomness or uncertainty makes us uncomfortable, then it's safe to assume that trafficking in randomness carries a degree of risk. To be blunt, the financial markets are risky! The stock market is even riskier!

There are two kinds of risk you must consider. The first is the risk that you lose money. If you purchase a single stock for $25 per share and it goes to $0, you have lost your entire investment. The second risk is volatility, or changes in the value of your portfolio over time. Volatility is risk, and volatility leads investors to make emotional decisions. The best way to describe the risk of volatility is to examine practical examples. The data that follows will help you understand the volatility and risk of investing in the financial markets.

The following show the historical returns and volatility expressed in standard deviation for various asset classes:

1-Year Government Bonds

Return	4.71%
Standard Deviation	1.72

Long-Term Corporate Bonds

Return	5.89%
Standard Deviation	7.33

High Yield Bonds

Return	6.81%
Standard Deviation	11.2

S&P 500 Index

Return	10.33%
Standard Deviation	21.64

U.S. Small Stocks

Return	12.61%
Standard Deviation	34.73

Standard deviation is a statistical measure used to express volatility around the averages of a portfolio. Standard deviation measures the dispersion or variation of returns of an asset, or the

Dennis P. Barba, Jr., Ph.D.

extent to which possible returns can vary from the arithmetic mean.

Typically, a portfolio will perform within one standard deviation approximately 68% of the time, and perform within two standard deviations approximately 95% of the time.

You will notice that the historical returns and standard deviation varied greatly from one asset class to another. In the extremes, short-term government bonds returned, on average, 4.71% per year with a standard deviation of 1.72, while Small Cap stocks averaged 12.61% with a standard deviation of 34.73.

How can these numbers help us examine potential risk? If we take the historical returns and standard deviations, we can develop a potential risk profile based on this historical data.

	Short-Term Government Bonds	SmallCap Stocks
Historical Return	4.71%	12.61%
Standard Deviation	1.71	34.73
First Standard Deviation	+6.42% to -3.00%	+47.34% to -22.12%
Second Standard Deviation	+8.13% to -4.71%	+82.07% to -56.85%

This means that an investor allocating funds in short-term government bonds should be able to accept a downside move of approximately 5%, while an investor in SmallCap stocks should be able to tolerate a loss of 50% in a single year.

More specifically, an investor in short-term government bonds should expect that approximately 68% of the time this investment should return between 6.42% and -3%. Additionally, approximately 95% of the time, this investor should expect to earn between 8.13% and -4.71%.

The investor in small cap stocks should expect that approximately 68% of the time this investment should return between 47.34% and -22.12%. Additionally, approximately 95% of the time this investor should expect to earn between 82.07% and -56.85%.

This math by no means guarantees a given level of volatility. However, the practice of using standard deviation to measure risk has been used for decades and, unfortunately, is rarely understood or used by most individual investors.

Maximum Decline Since 1926

1-Year Government Bonds
Maximum Decline   N/A

Long-Term Corporate Bonds
Maximum Decline   -22.37%

High Yield Bonds
Maximum Decline   -57.02%

S&P 500 Index
Maximum Decline   -83.41%

U.S. Small Stocks
Maximum Decline   -90.0%

The above data shows the maximum decline in excess of 10% since 1926 for various asset classes. You will notice that short-term government bonds have never suffered a decline of 10%. More importantly, you can see that investing in stocks can be quite risky. In the case of both LargeCap stocks (S&P 500) and U.S. small stocks, it is possible to lose a good portion of your wealth when things get ugly.

We can examine average returns and volatility for any time period. The following shows past returns and volatility of asset classes from 1979 to October 2005:

Returns & Volitility (1979 – 10, 2005)

1-Year Government Bonds
Return   8.80%
Standard Deviation   3.50

Long-Term Corporate Bonds
Return   10.07%
Standard Deviation   10.69

High Yield Bonds
Return   10.68%
Standard Deviation   9.32

S&P 500 Index
Return   15.11%
Standard Deviation   17.69

U.S. Small Stocks
Return   15.95%
Standard Deviation   23.66

You will again notice that the various asset classes have provided different degrees of return with varying degrees of risk (standard deviation).

Another good way to access volatility, is to examine how often various asset classes have exhibited different ranges of returns. In the following data you will notice that short-term bonds (Lehman Brothers 1-3 year government) have provided a positive return nearly 100% of the time, while large cap stocks (S&P 500) have provided a positive annual return approximately 84% of the time.

Similarly, short-term government bonds (Lehman Brothers 1-3 year government) have provided annual returns in excess of 10% approximately 33% of the time, while large cap stocks (S&P 500) have provided returns in excess of 10% approximately 68% of the time.

Range of Returns

1-Year Government Bonds

Return Greater than 10%	34%
Return Greater than 0%	100%

Long-Term Corporate Bonds

Return Greater than 10%	54%
Return Greater than 0%	81%

High Yield Bonds

Return Greater than 10%	49%
Return Greater than 0%	87%

S&P 500 Index

Return Greater than 10%	68%
Return Greater than 0%	84%

U.S. Small Stocks

Return Greater than 10%	65%
Return Greater than 0%	77%

Another good exercise in examining risk is to view the largest decline by decade. If we look at the 1980s, 1990s and 2000s we can view the maximum decline in excess of 10% by decade for each asset class. You will notice that in each decade there were significant declines in most asset classes.

Dennis P. Barba, Jr., Ph.D.

Maximum Decline in Excess of 10%

1-Year Government Bonds
Maximum Decline 1980s   N/A
Maximum Decline 1990s   N/A
Maximum Decline 2000s   N/A

Long-Term Corporate Bonds
Maximum Decline 1980s   -20%
Maximum Decline 1990s   N/A
Maximum Decline 2000s   -10%

High Yield Bonds
Maximum Decline 1980s   -10%
Maximum Decline 1990s   -17%
Maximum Decline 2000s   -12%

S&P 500 Index
Maximum Decline 1980s   -30%
Maximum Decline 1990s   -15%
Maximum Decline 2000s   -45%

U.S. Small Stocks
Maximum Decline 1980s   -33%
Maximum Decline 1990s   -31%
Maximum Decline 2000s   -28%

You should now have no problem agreeing with the statement that the financial markets are risky. The key is to understand this risk and attempt to develop a framework to deal with randomness.

While the concept of standard deviation and data mining for past performance is certainly helpful, it by no means guarantees that your holdings will not experience volatility that is more than you can stomach. As you have seen from the above charts, it is not uncommon for someone to lose between 25% and 50% of their money in equities during periods of extended declines. More importantly, there have been periods of sharp declines in certain securities the experts could not calculate. For example, on October 19, 1987 the Dow Jones Industrial Average fell approximately 29%. According to Benoit Mandelbrot, "the probability of that happening has odds so small that they have no meaning. It is a number outside the scale of nature."[20] Also, according to Mandelbrot and Hudson, "finance theory would predict that the Dow would experience daily swings in excess of 7% approximately once every 300,000 years. However, the Dow experienced daily swings in excess of 7% 48 times during the twentieth century."[21]

1998 was a particularly interesting year. Mandlebrot and Hudson outline: "The summer of 1998 presented investors with a series of worries: recession in Japan, possible devaluation in China, President Clinton facing impeachment and Russia facing a cash crunch. On August 4th, the Dow fell approximately 3.5%. Three weeks later the Dow fell by approximately 4.4% and on August 31st, stocks fell another 6.8%."[22] According to Mandelbrot and Hudson, "the odds of having three such declines in a single month were impossible - the odds of getting three such declines in the same month were approximately one in 500 billion." [23]

The point is the financial markets can and do experience price movements outside of the standard models of economic theory. More importantly, these extreme instances of volatility cannot be consistently and accurately predicted. They are random.

Volatility in the markets usually occurs **because** of some event or piece of information. According to Mandelbrot and Hudson, "the because is often something that comes from outside the market." [24]

A stock can drop **because** of an accounting scandal or a class-

[20] Benoit B. Mandelbrot & Richard L. Hudson, The *(mis) Behavior of Markets A Fractal View of Risk, Ruin, and Reward* (New York: Basic Books, 2004), p. 5.

[21] Benoit B. Mandelbrot & Richard L. Hudson, The *(mis) Behavior of Markets A Fractal View of Risk, Ruin, and Reward* (New York: Basic Books, 2004), p. 13.

[22] Benoit B. Mandelbrot & Richard L. Hudson, The *(mis) Behavior of Markets A Fractal View of Risk, Ruin, and Reward* (New York: Basic Books, 2004), p. 13.

[23] Benoit B. Mandelbrot & Richard L. Hudson, The *(mis) Behavior of Markets A Fractal View of Risk, Ruin, and Reward* (New York: Basic Books, 2004), p. 3.

[24] Benoit B. Mandelbrot & Richard L. Hudson, The *(mis) Behavior of Markets A Fractal View of Risk, Ruin, and Reward* (New York: Basic Books, 2004), p. 4.

Dennis P. Barba, Jr., Ph.D.

action lawsuit. A stock can drop **because** the company missed an earnings estimate. The market can drop **because** of the fear of inflation and interest rate increases. A stock can increase in value **because** a well-known investor or hedge fund manager has been acquiring shares.

You will notice that "**because**" is usually associated with an event that is **random, unexpected and unpredictable.**

It should now be obvious that the financial markets are risky. It is not uncommon for the market averages to experience significant and prolonged periods of negative performance. We have already discussed the fact that the average individual investor usually does far worse than the market averages. Therefore, it is safe to assume that it's not uncommon for many investors to "blow up" or "drive off the cliff."

The concept of "blowing up" or "driving off the cliff" is very important for individual investors to understand. There are two ways to "blow yourself up" or "drive off the cliff." First, you can simply lose all of your money through an excessive use of leverage, betting your entire fortune on one or a small number of stocks, continuously moving money from one losing investment to another, or several of the above combined with some bad luck. Eventually, you drive off the cliff, and when your car hits the ground you "blow up."

For most investors losing an entire fortune is uncommon. However, just because you don't "wipe yourself out" doesn't mean you haven't "blown up." When someone loses enough money that it has the potential to change their way of life, or they become so emotionally scarred that they are totally dominated by their emotions, they have "blown up."

The following are two examples. A 55-five-year-old professional with $1.2 million in his 401(k), who plans to retire at 60, has all of his money allocated in two SmallCap equity funds.

Over the course of 18 months, these two funds lose 50% of their value. Now nearly 57, he has lost approximately half of his life savings in a short period of time. His ability to retire by age 60 is nearly impossible. He "blew-up" by being under diversified and losing a substantial sum of money fairly quickly. In all likelihood, he never thought it was possible for his 401(k) account to fall 50% in less than two years. Remember, we are largely influenced by our recent memories and experiences. Since this investor was familiar with these fund holdings increasing in value almost monthly for several years, there was no thought given to the possibility this trend may reverse.

Let's examine an example of someone much younger. A 35-year-old professional has managed to save $200,000. She invests this entire sum of money in the stock market and within one year has lost 25% of her portfolio. Since her only and most recent experience with investing in stocks is negative, she sells everything and vows to never put any of her money into stocks again. She places all of her future savings into savings accounts and certificates of deposit. At this time, she has "blown herself up" mentally, as it pertains to investing. It is likely she will need to earn a significant return on her savings in order to fund her retirement. By driving off the cliff the first time she invested, she now mentally locks herself into accepting low returns. What if savings account and CD rates are insufficient to fund her retirement? How will she achieve financial independence in retirement?

CHAPTER 8

What Do We Do?

You should have learned some important lessons up to this point.

1. Most of us under-save.

2. Most of us underperform the market averages.

3. The returns of the market, individual securities, mutual funds and money managers are random and hard to predict.

4. Investing in the financial markets is risky.

5. We are driven by our emotions, and the risk of the financial markets makes it more difficult to control our emotions.

If investing is so risky and our emotions are so hard to control, then why invest at all? The answer to this question is simple. Nearly all of us need to earn a significant return on our savings in order to have any realistic chance of funding our retirement. The fact that most of us under-save makes earning a return on our assets even more important. The less we save, the more important the return becomes.

Earlier in the book we questioned if your objective should be to "beat the market." Should your investment objective be to beat the market or some given benchmark? This is not an easy question to answer.

When determining your investment objective, it is best to rely on a clearly defined strategy as opposed to relying on your emotions or a gut feeling. In short, you will need to manage to a clearly defined set of objectives designed to help you achieve your financial goals.

The return your friends or neighbors earn on their investments is irrelevant to your situation. Remember, most people exaggerate their returns anyway, so take their statements of investment genius with a grain of salt.

Dennis P. Barba, Jr., Ph.D.

Likewise, to state that your objective is to "beat the market" without knowing what you are trying to accomplish financially, is nothing more than an emotional statement. This type of investing will likely lead to assuming more investment risk than you can stomach.

Remember the word "**Because**." Be careful how you use this word when stating your investment objectives. "I want to earn in excess of 11% per year **Because** my friend Ted has averaged 11% during the past 10 years." "I want to beat the market **Because** hardly anyone else can, and I am certainly smarter than everyone else." I want to earn 12% **Because** I have a gut feeling that this is what is necessary to fund my retirement." The word **Because** in the above statements is largely based on your emotions. This type of behavior will help set you up for failure.

The Need for Growth

Unfortunately, most of us need our assets to grow in order to have a realistic chance to retire. If we want to retire and maintain any semblance of our pre-retirement lifestyle, we will likely have to generate growth well in excess of what banks will pay us on our savings.

One of the primary objectives in financial planning is to figure out what range of returns is necessary to fund our financial goals.

We still have to answer the question of "should I try to beat the market?" The answer to this question is "it depends." This depends on what return is necessary to fund your financial objectives.

The return necessary to achieve financial success, combined with your tolerance for risk, is what should drive your investment decisions.

Since most of us need to make our money grow in order to

retire, how do we figure out the necessary return? Unfortunately, this is not a simple question. If you cut corners trying to answer this question, you can set yourself up for failure.

In the introduction of this book I stated that long-term financial success could be achieved by the following:

- Clearly defining your goals.

- Identifying the return necessary to achieve your goals.

- Defining your tolerance for risk.

- Developing, implementing and refining a strategic plan for the management of your assets.

CHAPTER 9

Clearly Defining Your Goals & Identifying the Return Necessary to Achieve Your Goals

"If you do not know where you are going you are already lost." This quote certainly applies to many aspects of our personal and professional lives. However, this particularly holds true as it applies to investing our money. Without the proper knowledge of our goals, how can we possibly know what to do with our investments?

Fortunately, identifying our goals should not be that difficult. For most of us, our primary financial goal is to retire at some point in the future.

Making the decision that we would like to retire by a certain age is not difficult to figure out. Making it happen is another story.

One of the best ways to show how to determine the return necessary to retire is to use an example.

The following example of the Sample family will show how to determine the return necessary to fund retirement:

- Both 59 years old.

- Wish to retire at age 65.

- Mr. Sample makes $85,000 annually and is currently saving 10% of his income into a 401(k) plan. His current 401(k) balance is $375,000.

- Mrs. Sample makes $35,000 annually and is likewise saving 10% of her salary into a 401(k) plan. Her current 401(k) balance is $200,000.

- Mr. Sample is anticipating receiving Social Security benefits of $19,000 annually at retirement. Mr. Sample also has a $1,000 per month pension benefit commencing at age 65.

- Mrs. Sample is anticipating receiving Social Security

benefits of $14,000 annually and has no pension benefits.

- Mr. Sample has an Individual Retirement Account (IRA) with a current balance of $120,000 and anticipates making the maximum allowable contribution prior to retirement.

- Mrs. Sample has an Individual Retirement Account (IRA) with a current balance of $50,000 and anticipates making the maximum allowable contribution prior to retirement.

- Mr. and Mrs. Sample have $50,000 in a savings account.

- The Sample's have a home valued at $300,000, which will be paid for at age 60. They do not anticipate selling their house during retirement.

- The Samples believe they need the equivalent of $7,000 in monthly, after-tax income to fund retirement. Please note this figure is expressed in today's dollars.

- The Samples are projecting that their living expenses will inflate at an annual rate of 3%.

- The Samples have no debt other than their mortgage, which will be paid off in two years.

The case of the Samples is fairly typical and uncomplicated.

Current investment assets	$ 795,000
Real estate	$ 300,000
Net Worth	$1,095,000

The Samples are millionaires! They should be on easy street! What's the problem if they have $1 million and no debt? At this point we don't know if there's a problem, but we are going to find out. This is the purpose of our analysis. The Samples are not sure if they can retire at age 65 and have the income necessary to fund retirement.

One item of importance is to factor in the 3% rate of inflation.

When they retire at age 65 they will need approximately $97,379 in annual income, or $8,115 per month after-tax, to purchase what $7,000 purchases today.

More importantly, when the Samples are 75, assuming a 3% rate of inflation, they will need approximately $130,000, or $10,833 per month after-tax, to purchase what $7,000 purchases today.

Taking inflation into consideration is a very important component in attempting to determine the return necessary to fund your goals. This is one of the most overlooked assumptions in financial planning.

At this point, the Samples have a target date for retirement and they know how much money they are going to need each year during retirement. Equally important, they have an understanding of how their income needs may increase with inflation as they age.

Next, the Samples need to figure out what return or range of returns is necessary to accomplish their objective of retirement by age 65.

The Samples desire to be somewhat conservative with their portfolio and are concerned about volatility. A portfolio decline of 20% in a single year would devastate Mrs. Sample emotionally, and Mr. Sample likewise states that a large decline in a single year would make him extremely nervous.

The Samples want to examine the feasibility of adopting a moderately conservative investment posture with approximately 60% of their portfolio in bonds and 40% in stocks. Their targeted rate of return will be approximately 8%.

Assuming this type of allocation can average 8% annually, will the Samples be able to achieve their retirement objectives? Let's take a closer look.

Assuming this portfolio averages exactly 8.17% each year from today thorough age 92, the Samples would be able to fund their inflation-adjusted living expenses and still have a surplus of approximately $2 million left in their estate.

Once again, at this point most people think they have a recipe for long-term success, and that they have no retirement issues. After all, their financial plan shows a $2 million surplus.

The biggest mistake in assuming the Samples have a worry-free retirement is the assumption that they will earn 8.17% each year. Financial planning programs typically assume the average return is achieved each and every year in succession. However, in reality this is impossible. The odds of a portfolio consisting of 60% bonds and 40% stocks earning exactly 8.17% each and every year are near zero. It is statistically impossible for this to occur.

What can we do to help determine if this type of portfolio allocation will work?

Although there is no exact science that will guarantee success, we can use statistical analysis to determine the odds of success.

There are three main methods one can use to help determine odds of success.

- What if analysis

- Stress testing or sensitivity analysis

- Monte Carlo analysis

What If Analysis

"What If" analysis is exactly as it sounds. What if something does not go as planned? For example, what if the Sample's portfolio loses 10% when the Samples are age 65 and another

10% when they are age 66? In short, what happens if their portfolio suffers a two-year drawdown of 20%?

For the Samples, this "What If" scenario would have significant consequences. Assuming this 20% drawdown occurred, the samples would run out of funds just prior to age 92. Their surplus would evaporate. This drawdown could lead to a $2,000,000 swing in the wrong direction.

You should examine as many different scenarios with your assumptions as you think are necessary. Some good examples are as follows:

- What if we save less than projected?

- What if we want to retire earlier or later?

- What if we sell our house, downsize and reinvest the difference into our portfolio?

- What if the market suffers a significant decline?

- What if I switch jobs and lose my pension benefit?

- What happens if we increase or decrease our desired retirement income needs?

Stress Testing or Sensitivity Analysis

What we are trying to determine are the possible shortfalls in our planning assumptions. We can use sensitivity analysis on the asset classes or investments we are going to use to fund our portfolio.

In the Sample's example, they are contemplating allocating their portfolio 60% in bonds and 40% in equities. Remember, their plan is assuming they earn the average of 8.17% each and every year. We have already stated this will not occur.

The assumptions the Sample's are using for their bond asset

class returns range from 5.4% for short-term bonds up to 7.73% for long-term bonds.

Likewise, the equity return assumptions the Samples are using range from 11% for international stocks to 13.5% for U.S. Small Cap stocks.

We use sensitivity analysis to see what would happen to the Samples if the actual returns ware significantly below their historical projections.

We will now assume the actual return of the Sample's bond asset classes will range from 4.5% for short-term bonds to 6.75% for long-term bonds.

Likewise, we will now assume the actual return of the Sample's equity asset classes will be 8% across the board, meaning that no equity sector will exceed an annualized return of 8% going forward.

How will the changes in the return assumptions for bonds and equities change the Sample's ability to fund their retirement?

Once again, their surplus is wiped out. Additionally, the Samples would likely run out of money in their mid-to-late-80s.

Simply using sensitivity analysis to assume the actual asset class returns may be less than the historical or projected returns is likewise not sufficient in determining if the Samples can retire.

The software program is again assuming that the portfolio is earning the average of the revised asset class returns each and every year in succession. In real life this cannot occur.

As discussed, even if you earn the average return you are projecting, over a long period of time, there is no guarantee you will not run out of funds. Two families can have the same financial goals and each average the same annualized return over a 30-year period of time. However, depending on the variation or sequence of returns, one family may actually run out of funds.

Monte Carlo Analysis

Monte Carlo analysis can be used to calculate the different sequences of possible returns of your portfolio. Monte Carlo software runs simulations using random variables to show how variations in rates of return each year can affect your odds of success. Depending on the Monte Carlo application you use to perform this analysis, you can calculate the possible results of your assumptions by running the potential outcomes between 1,000 and over 100,000 times, each time using a different sequence of assumptions or returns. The software can literally run every conceivable combination of either past returns or the assumptions you are using to search for instances of failure.

Monte Carlo simulations produce a range of possible results, some successful and some unsuccessful.

Monte Carlo analysis is an important tool in financial analysis. As we have discussed, it is impossible to earn your desired rate of return each and every year. Additionally, even if you average your desired average rate of return over a long period of time, you can still run out of funds, depending on the sequence of your returns. Monte Carlo analysis can provide a more realistic picture of your odds of success by factoring randomness into your assumptions.

In the case of the Samples, the Monte Carlo analysis predicts their odds of success at 75%.

What should the Samples conclude? It seems as if their planning shows they will have fairly good odds of success. The different statistical tests show them having enough money to last into their mid-80s on the low side and having a $2 million surplus on the high side.

The answer to this question depends on the Samples willingness to accept the random chance they may fail. What if they live into their mid-90s and remain fairly active? What if the markets experience more volatility than normal? What if they wish to leave an estate for their children?

The Samples decide that 75% odds of success are not acceptable. As a result, they decide they are willing to become more aggressive, with the hope of earning a higher return. How do the Samples determine how aggressive they should become? They know they need to earn at least 8% per year in order to achieve their goals, but they are fairly confident that keeping 60% of their portfolio in bonds could hinder their ability to hit their target.

What should the Samples do next?

Dennis P. Barba, Jr., Ph.D.

CHAPTER 10

Diversification & the Asset Allocation Decision – Your Emotional Tolerance Level®

We will continue using the Samples as a case study. The Samples have come a long way since defining their goals. The Samples have determined that they need to earn at least 8% percent in order to be able to fund their retirement.

If designed and implemented correctly, an efficient asset allocation strategy can help to manage your emotions. Earlier in this book we covered the tendencies of individual investors to make emotional-based investment decisions that contribute to investor underperformance.

When developing your asset allocation strategy, it is important for you to determine your Emotional Tolerance Level®. Your Emotional Tolerance Level® is the level of portfolio volatility you can take before your emotions take over and dominate investment decisions.

For example, someone reads about the possibility of an influenza pandemic and immediately converts his or her entire portfolio into cash. Why might this be a bad idea?

- **Transaction costs** – This decision will likely cost you a significant amount of expense in terms of transaction costs.

- **Tax consequences** – You may have to pay a significant amount of taxes on your gains.

- **Potential lost returns** – What if the impetus of your emotional decision does not materialize? You may be grateful that you are still wealthy. However, if your portfolio had increased in value how you would recoup this lost return? Unfortunately, many times we attempt to recoup these lost returns by implementing an even more aggressive strategy to make up for our last emotional mistake. Interestingly, the decision to become more aggressive is as emotional as our initial decision to abandon ship!

Dennis P. Barba, Jr., Ph.D.

- **When to return to the market** – How precisely will you know when to re-enter the market? You have already made the emotional decision to sell everything. You then made another emotional decision to become more aggressive as a result of your first emotional decision. Now, you must decide when to put your money back "in play." This will probably not occur until another emotional reaction causes you to "pull the trigger."

You should be getting the point by now, and for many, this may sound familiar.

So how can you come up with an idea of your ***Emotional Tolerance Level*®**? Again, you are attempting to determine what level of portfolio volatility you can handle before you are unable to control your emotions.

The best way to accomplish this is to closely examine the statistical characteristics of any contemplated investment strategy. What you are trying to determine is how bad things could get with your proposed strategy, as well as if you can stay the course when things do get bad.

We will continue with the case of Mr. and Mrs. Sample. If you remember, the Samples initially thought a portfolio composed of 60% bonds and 40% stocks would achieve their objectives. However, after their initial analysis, the Samples are now willing to consider becoming more aggressive. They are still concerned that a portfolio decline in excess of 20% could cause them to begin acting on their emotions.

The Samples were initially considering a portfolio consisting of the following asset classes.

U.S. one-year government bonds	20%
Lehman Brothers Aggregate Bond Index	40%
S&P 500 Index	20%

S&P MidCap 400 Index	5%
Russell 2000 Index	5%
MSCI EAFE Foreign Index	10%

This asset allocation mix would represent a diversified portfolio that is arguably better diversified than the vast majority of individual investors. However, the Samples are not completely confident this allocation mix will provide the returns necessary to fund retirement.

The Samples examined past performance data to see what would have happened if they were invested in these asset classes. The following were examined from 1981 through the first quarter of 2006.

Average Return	10.79%
Standard Deviation	7.60
1-year return	10.10%
3-year average return	13.24%
5-year average return	6.90%
7-year average return	6.15%
10-year average return	7.91%

This portfolio suffered two declines during this 24-year period in excess of 10%. The biggest loss was from September 2002 though June 2003 when this portfolio would have lost approximately 10.5%. The Samples feel good about the fact this portfolio only suffered a maximum decline of 10% during this 24-year period. They remember 1987 and the bear market of 2000-2002, and saw many of their friends wiped out during these times. They are comfortable that this asset allocation strategy would have only lost a fraction of what the market lost during the previous large declines. The Samples make a decision to examine the maximum decline of all portfolios under consideration and to make certain they are comfortable with the volatility associated with their choice.

The average long-term return of 10.79% and the historical levels of volatility fit within the Samples emotional tolerance level. Even including three of the worst years in the history of U.S. equity markets, this portfolio has averaged nearly 8%.

This asset allocation strategy for the Samples was created using the principles of Modern Portfolio Theory. Many investment professionals rely on Modern Portfolio Theory to generate their portfolio allocations.

Modern Portfolio Theory looks at the detailed historical behavior of different asset classes. In a given set of market conditions, some asset classes will outperform the market and others will underperform. Modern Portfolio Theory uses statistical analysis to evaluate different combinations of asset classes to determine the most efficient combination for a given level of risk.

The three components used in Modern Portfolio Theory to create portfolios are:

- Expected Return

- Standard Deviation

- Correlation

These components can be used to generate an efficiently allocated portfolio via a mathematical process called Mean Variance Optimization (MVO). MVO is used to attempt to identify the portfolios that have the least amount of risk (standard deviation) for a given level of return.

The use of Modern Portfolio Theory and MVO, while not perfect, is significantly more strategic than what the vast majority of individual investors, and arguably financial advisors, use to implement their investment strategies.

One potential flaw with Modern Portfolio Theory is the analysis assumes the three components: expected return, standard deviation and correlation are known. While they may well be known in terms of what has happened in the past, they are not known with certainty going forward.

We have already stated that it's impossible to earn your expected rate of return each and every year in succession. It's likewise near impossible for a portfolio constructed using Modern Portfolio Theory to exhibit the exact characteristics of the projected expected return, standard deviation and correlations.

Relying solely on the past to base your investment decisions has tended to cause investors to overweight the asset classes that were the best performing in the past. Due to the emotions of both investors and financial advisors, there's a tendency to end up with non-diversified or under-diversified asset allocation strategies.

Thus, the Samples still have some work to do if they want to create an efficiently allocated portfolio designed to be within their Emotional Tolerance Level®.

Mean Variance Optimization does not include any factors for randomness. Monte Carlo analysis, on the other hand, is designed to take randomness into consideration.

One option for the Samples is to simply plug the expected returns, correlations and standard deviations of the past into a Monte Carlo analyzer and determine the odds of success. This is, in effect, what we did earlier with the Samples.

As we have already stated, classic Mean Variance Optimization assumes the investor knows what the returns and volatility will be going forward. In the real world both are random.

The Samples make an appointment to see a financial advisor

who specializes in asset allocation strategies.

After reviewing the Sample's existing planning documents, the adviser explains to the couple that the problem lies in the return assumptions being used in their original scenario. The advisor recommends their asset allocation strategy include an analysis using forward-looking return assumptions. The advisor explains that they should consider what is expected to happen in the future relative to equity and fixed income returns. He explains that current bond yields are well below the historical range of 5.4% to nearly 8% the Samples are using. Likewise, he explains that the 11% to 13.5% assumptions for equities likewise may be overly optimistic.

He suggests that in addition to the stress testing the Samples performed on their historical assumptions, that they create an allocation model based on forward-looking assumptions.

The Samples agree to let the advisor perform this analysis.

The forward-looking capital market assumptions used for the Samples asset classes are as follows:

Short-Term Bonds	4.49%
Intermediate-Term Bonds	5.51%
S&P 500	11.07%
S&P MidCap 400	10.17%
Russell 2000	10.48%
MSCI EAFE Foreign Index	11.28%

What can we do to figure out a new asset allocation strategy?

We use an optimizer program that re-samples or performs a Monte Carlo analysis using the forward-looking asset class assumptions.

We will use optimization software to Monte Carlo our expected returns, correlations and standard deviations. This Monte Carlo analysis will draw parameters that are calculated by our forward-looking assumptions, not from the historical data itself.

This analysis is important because the Monte Carlo program can draw from any possible occurrences, not just those based on what happened in the past. Additionally, we are using data based on what we believe will occur in the future, not just on what occurred in the past.

This can result in an analysis that creates more realistic results.

We use the same asset classes as the previous analysis. However, prior to running the analysis, we place some constraints on the asset classes to be certain we have a diversified portfolio.

We tell the analyzer program that each equity asset class has to have a minimum allocation of 7% and a maximum of 30%. Likewise, each fixed income asset class must have a minimum allocation of 10% and a maximum of 60%.

We then perform an analysis that re-samples our assumptions

Dennis P. Barba, Jr., Ph.D.

to search for the most efficient asset allocation mixes for each level of risk. The analyzer concludes that the following asset allocation mix is the most efficient for an expected return of 8%:

Short-Term Bonds	25%
Intermediate-Term Bonds	10%
S&P 500	23.45%
S&P MidCap 400	7%
Russell 2000	18.66%
MSCI EAFE Foreign Index	15.89%

The analyzer program provides some very important statistical data that will help the Samples determine if this mix fits within their Emotional Tolerance Level®.

This data is as follows:

Expected Return	8.37%
Standard Deviation	9.73
Return Threshold	4.15%
Probability	66.77%

Interpreting this data helps the Samples draw the following conclusions:

The expected return of this portfolio is 8.37% which fits within the Samples range of returns.

This portfolio has odds of approximately 66.77% that the minimum return during any single year will be at least 4.15%.

The standard deviation is 9.73. This is still significantly below the average standard deviation (17.5) of the market or S&P 500 index.

The Samples should expect this portfolio to average between -1.36% and 18.10% approximately 68% of the time. Likewise, the Samples should expect this portfolio to average between -11.09% and 27.83% approximately 95% of the time. This means that the odds of their portfolio declining in excess of 11% in a single year appear to be approximately 5%.

Return Percentiles:

	1yr	3yr	5yr	7yr	10yr	20yr	30yr
80th	16.38	12.73	11.63	11.05	10.54	9.77	9.43
50th	7.93	7.93	7.93	7.93	7.93	7.93	7.93
10th	-3.77	1.01	2.53	3.35	4.08	5.2	5.69
5th	-6.85	-0.87	1.05	2.09	4.43	5.07	5.45

The Monte Carlo analysis created a Return Percentiles chart. This information can be useful in determining your Emotional Tolerance Level®. For example, in any single year there is a 20% chance of achieving a 16.38% return or higher. Likewise, in any single year there are 5% odds of having a -6.85% return or lower.

The Samples also examined the past performance of this revised asset allocation strategy.

They found that the worst 12-month period of performance from 1981 would have been approximately -10%. Likewise, they found that the worst consecutive decline (drawdown) since 1981 would have been approximately -18% from November 1987 through January 1989. The Samples again take comfort that even this more aggressive portfolio did not suffer a 20% decline in a single year. Moreover, over a 24-year period, the portfolio did not experience a consecutive decline of 20%.

As a result of their analysis, the Samples decide they will become more aggressive and hold a portfolio consisting of approximately 35% in bonds and 65% in stocks.

The Samples have used a variety of historical and forward-looking analyses, in combination with a detailed Monte Carlo analysis, to help determine their course of action.

The Samples also examined what would have occurred had they been investing in this portfolio since 1981. The following is what they discovered.

- Annualized return - 1981   11.47%

- Standard deviation   11.57%

- Maximum drawdown   -18%

- Return 1 year   21.87%

- Annualized return 3 years   19.60%

- Annualized return 5 years   7.60%

- Annualized return 7 years   6.50%

- Annualized return 10 years   8.62%

- The portfolio had a positive annual return approximately 84% of the time.

- The portfolio achieved an annual return in excess of 10% approximately 59% of the time.

After their anaysis, they felt they had to become more aggressive in order to maintain thier origional ritirement goal of age 65. Likewise, both the historical and projected ranges of volatility and odds of achieving various returns fit within their Emotional Tolerance Level®.

As we have discussed, they now have to find securities to implement this strategy. Developing an asset allocation strategy is only half the battle. The Samples need to work with a professional to select securities that fit within the profile of their stated asset allocation strategy. This is no easy task and will take a great deal of time on the part of the Samples and their advisor. Very few advisors or stockbrokers specialize in this type of analysis. Again, most rely on emotions when choosing investments, or simply sell based on performance. Allocating your funds based solely on what performed well recently, will subject your returns to luck and excess randomness.

An important lesson to learn from the Samples is that being unemotional and investing via a clear strategy takes time and a good deal of hard work. The analyses conducted in this example were used by implementing sophisticated statistical analytical tools. It is important to find a professional who cannot only help you determine your goals, but also help you develop a plan for implementation.

The same type of statistical analysis would have to be conducted to develop an implementation plan. We will not go through the details of this implementation in this book, as you should by now understand the importance of developing an investment strategy via understanding what has happened, what could happen and what is likely to occur. You will need to understand the statistical characteristics of any combination of securities you use to implement an asset allocation strategy. In the beginning of this book we outlined how difficult it is for the vast majority of money managers to beat the market or a specific benchmark index. Therefore, it is critical you work with someone who is able to not only understand how to develop an asset-class-based asset allocation strategy, but likewise is able to conduct the analysis necessary to implement your strategy while providing measurable value.

Chapter 11

Guidelines for Asset Allocation

The last chapter went into some sophisticated and complicated mathematical methods to develop an efficiently allocated portfolio. It is important to understand that 100% certainty in terms of what your returns will be or how they will vary is impossible through any technique. Ultimately, no matter how much research you conduct, you cannot precisely forecast randomness.

While no methodology is perfect, this type of strategy for developing your asset allocation goes far beyond what most individual investors will commit to enduring. This is in direct contrast to being an emotional investor. This takes time, and this time gives us the chance to better manage our emotions.

The reason many of you are reading this book is to hopefully get some ideas on how to allocate your investment assets. The following will give some guidelines on a basic asset allocation strategy for various levels of risk.

Please note, these models are at the asset class level. Most individual investors will fail to do the necessary research to develop an asset class model to begin the asset allocation process. Once you agree on the asset classes that will make up your asset allocation strategy, you still must choose the investments for each asset class. This can be done in a variety of ways.

- Mutual Funds

- Individual Stocks and Fixed Income Securities

- Separate Account or Money Managers

- Index Funds

Once again, it is imperative you work with a professional to help implement your asset allocation plan. A professional should help you implement an asset allocation plan that is consistent with your return objectives and level of risk. The securities selected to implement your asset allocation strategy should have the statistical characteristics of the model you choose.

Model-Based Allocation Strategies

The following models provide general guidelines in today's market environment for investors in five broad categories, in terms of risk:

- Conservative

- Moderately Conservative

- Moderate

- Moderately Aggressive

- Aggressive

These benchmarks provide efficient levels of volatility as expressed in standard deviation for each classification of risk. Likewise, each model provides targeted levels of expected return. Each investor should be comfortable with each classification of risk.

The Emotional Tolerance Level* takes into effect each portfolio experiencing negative returns into the second standard deviation for three consecutive years. Although the odds of this occurring are less than five percent, and the following asset class combinations have never experienced such a drawdown, an investor should be able to tolerate such a decline. As discussed, drawdowns are random, as are the length and severity of each drawdown. Since the odds of such a drawdown exist, an investor should be prepared to tolerate such a decline.

Conservative

LargeCap Equity	**13%**
Small/MidCap Equity	**2%**
International Equity	**5%**
Short-Term Bonds	**55%**
Intermediate-Term Bonds	**15%**
International Bonds	**5%**

Expected Return	_5.5% to 7%_
Maximum Standard Deviation	_4.5_

Emotional Tolerance Level Considerations

Amount of one-year return you should be able to accept: **-5%**

Amount of consecutive drawdown you should be able to accept over a longer period of time (approximately three years):

-11% to -15%

Moderately Conservative

LargeCap Equity	24%
Small/MidCap Equity	6%
International Equity	10%
Short-Term Bonds	30%
Intermediate-Term Bonds	20%
International Bonds	10%

Expected Return	_7.5 % to 8.5%_
Maximum Standard Deviation	6.5

Emotional Tolerance Level Considerations

Amount of one-year return you should be able to accept: **-6%**

Amount of consecutive drawdown you should be able to accept over a longer period of time (approximately three years):

-15% to -18%

Moderate

LargeCap Equity	32%
Small/MidCap Equity	14%
International Equity	14%
Short-Term Bonds	25%
Intermediate-Term Bonds	20%
International Bonds	5%

Expected Return	_8.0% to 10.5%_
Maximum Standard Deviation	_9_

Emotional Tolerance Level Considerations

Amount of one-year return you should be able to accept: **-10%**

Amount of consecutive drawdown you should be able to accept over a longer period of time (approximately three years):

-25% to -30%

Moderately Aggressive

LargeCap Equity	**40%**
Small/MidCap Equity	**17%**
International Equity	**18%**
Short-Term Bonds	**10%**
Intermediate-Term Bonds	**10%**
International Bonds	**5%**

Expected Return	_10% to 11%_
Maximum Standard Deviation	_12_

Emotional Tolerance Level Considerations

Amount of one-year return you should be able to accept: **-15%**

Amount of consecutive drawdown you should be able to accept over a longer period of time (approximately three years):

-30% to -45%

Aggressive

LargeCap Equity	43%
Small/MidCap Equity	25%
International Equity	22%
Short-Term Bonds	0%
Intermediate-Term Bonds	5%
International Bonds	5%

Expected Return	_11% to 13%_
Maximum Standard Deviation	14

Emotional Tolerance Level Considerations

Amount of one-year return you should be able to accept: **-20%**

Amount of consecutive drawdown you should be able to accept over a longer period of time (approximately three years):

-50% to 60%

Although a great deal of statistical analysis has been completed to develop these models, the expected return and volatility at each level of risk is not guaranteed. It is very important that you understand and are comfortable with the range of volatility for each classification of risk.

By understanding your Emotional Tolerance Level,[®] you will be much more likely to stay in the game, and not only stick with, but consistently rebalance your portfolio.

The Importance of Rebalancing

The assumptions we have discussed for the Sample family, as well as the model portfolio allocations, assume you rebalance your portfolio annually.

Implementing an asset allocation strategy that corresponds with your desired returns and your Emotional Tolerance Level® is a significant achievement. However, this does not mean you should never look at your portfolio again. As time moves forward, you will discover that the weighting of each asset class and investment in your portfolio will change. Over time, the asset classes and related holdings in your portfolio will each earn a different return. This will result in asset class weights that are inconsistent with your original allocation strategy, and this is completely normal.

What does rebalancing mean and why should you rebalance? Portfolio rebalancing is the process of buying and selling positions within your portfolio to make certain the asset class weightings are consistent with your stated asset allocation strategy.

Your asset class weights will change as a result of the variations in returns of your investments. Therefore, the actual percentage of your portfolio assets allocated to each sector will change over time. Depending on how severe the change, your portfolio may become subject to risk characteristics that are inconsistent with your stated asset allocation strategy. Quite simply, because of certain asset classes becoming overweighed, your portfolio risk characteristics may become inconsistent with your Emotional Tolerance Level®.

We will once again return to the case of the Samples. The Samples portfolio consists of the following asset classes and percentages:

Short-Term Bonds	25%
Intermediate-Term Bonds	10%
S&P 500	23.45%
S&P MidCap 400	7%
Russell 2000	18.66%
MSCI EAFE Foreign Index	15.89%

Assuming the Samples invested $100,000 into their portfolio, the dollar amount per asset class would be as follows.

Initial portfolio value

Short-Term Bonds	$25,000
Intermediate-Term Bonds	$10,000
S&P 500	$23,450
S&P MidCap 400	$ 7,000
Russell 2000	$18,660
MSCI EAFE Foreign Index	$15,890

At the end of the first year, the Samples find that the equity asset class components of their portfolio dramatically outperformed the fixed income components. This has caused a change in their allocation of asset classes, increasing the percentage they originally allocated in equities, while decreasing the amount allocated in fixed income securities.

Value after end of first year

Short-Term Bonds	$26,000
Intermediate-Term Bonds	$10,450
S&P 500	$28,609
S&P MidCap 400	$ 9,450
Russell 2000	$23,706
MSCI EAFE Foreign Index	$19,068

The Sample s portfolio grew from $100,000 to $117,283 in one year. As you will notice, the equity asset classes dramatically outperformed the fixed income asset classes. As a result, there is more weight in equities than the original asset allocation strategy called for.

Most people would be willing to leave the asset mix as is for the time being. You would have been comfortable with the steady increase in account value.

Additionally, investors tend to have a problem selling securities that are up in value, and buying more of something that is not performing as well. It's important to understand that not rebalancing a well-diversified portfolio, could result in over-weighting the riskier asset classes. There could be consequences later as a result of not rebalancing today.

Let's continue with the Samples We will compare the values of their rebalanced portfolio against a portfolio left unchanged.

At the end of the second year, LargeCap equities and foreign equities take a beating, SmallCap and MidCap equities lose a modest amount and fixed income securities have another good year of performance.

Asset class performance for year two

Short-Term Bonds	+ 6%
Intermediate-Term Bonds	+ 7%
S&P 500	- 28%
S&P MidCap 400	- 11%
Russell 2000	- 13%
MSCI EAFE Foreign Index	- 25%

The following will compare the second year performance of the rebalanced portfolio versus the non-rebalanced portfolio.

Rebalanced portfolio

Initial rebalanced portfolio allocations

Short-Term Bonds	$29,320
Intermediate-Term Bonds	$11,729
S&P 500	$27,505
S&P MidCap 400	$ 8,210
Russell 2000	$21,887
MSCI EAFE Foreign Index	$18,637

The above is how the account should have been rebalanced at the beginning of the second year. The account value at the beginning of the second year was $117,291.

Value of rebalanced portfolio at end of year two

Short-Term Bonds	$31,080
Intermediate-Term Bonds	$12,608
S&P 500	$19,802
S&P MidCap 400	$ 7,307
Russell 2000	$19,040
MSCI EAFE Foreign Index	$13,997
Ending Portfolio Value	$103,814
Loss for the year	-11.48%

Non-rebalanced portfolio

Initial non-rebalanced portfolio allocations

Short-Term Bonds	$26,000
Intermediate-Term Bonds	$10,450
S&P 500	$28,609
S&P MidCap 400	$ 9,450
Russell 2000	$23,706
MSCI EAFE Foreign Index	$19,068

The above are the ending values of each asset class at the end of year one assuming the portfolio was not rebalanced at the beginning of year two. Again, the beginning account value at the beginning of the second year was $117,291.

Value of non-rebalanced portfolio at end of year two

Short-Term Bonds	$27,560
Intermediate-Term Bonds	$11,234
S&P 500	$20,598
S&P MidCap 400	$ 8,411
Russell 2000	$20,624
MSCI EAFE Foreign Index	$14,301
Ending Portfolio Value	$102,728
Loss for the year	-12.41%

Over the course of just one year, the Samples would have given up approximately 1% by not rebalancing their portfolio. This may not seem like very much. However, if you repeat this pattern several times over the long term, it can greatly diminish your odds of success. Moreover, if you fail to rebalance for an extended period of time, and your asset classes become severely skewed toward the riskier asset classes, the results can be devastating. Unfortunately, many investors experienced the effects of being under-diversified during the early part of this decade.

If you are going to spend the time developing and implementing an asset allocation strategy, it makes sense to adhere to the rebalancing strategy used in your assumptions.

Finally, an asset allocation strategy is dynamic. As economic conditions and conditions in your life change, so should your asset allocation strategy.

You should make sure to work with a specialist who is well versed in creating efficient asset allocation strategies. Many investors have communicated that it's difficult to determine if

Dennis P. Barba, Jr., Ph.D.

a financial advisor really knows much about asset allocation. You should be cognizant of the fact that asset allocation and diversification became unpopular during the 1990s. It's important to deal with an expert who remained objective during this time period and adhered to their fundamental principles, as opposed to chasing performance and selling "what's hot."

Ultimately, you are trying to determine if the person you are considering understands and embraces these concepts, or if he or she simply follows the guidelines of their firm's research department. The following are some things you should look for when selecting the person or firm to develop and implement your asset allocation strategy.

- How long have you been in the business?

- What is your process for developing an asset allocation strategy?

- How long have you been developing and implementing efficient asset allocation strategies? You want to make certain this person has been practicing these principals for many years, not just since asset allocation became popular again since the 2000-2002 declines. Ask for references to verify this answer.

- How does your process differ from the average financial advisor?

- What value can you can add to my investment process?

- How often do you change your asset class recommendations? What causes you to make an asset class change?

- What is your policy on portfolio rebalancing and why?

- How do you select the securities that are used to implement your asset allocation strategies? Please outline the investment selection process. What you want to avoid is someone who simply sells you a product that is designed to diversify your portfolio via a firm-directed strategy. You are looking for experts, not "drinkers of the corporate Kool Aid."

- What statistical methods/tools do you use to help create and implement your work?

To summarize, it is important you deal with an expert in this area. You must conduct your due diligence when interviewing a professional to help you become an unemotional investor. Search for the professional who can tell you what they do and why they do it. Likewise, be sure this person is an independent thinker and understands their methodology and is not just a follower of his or her firm's corporate directives.

CHAPTER 12
Conclusion

I want to end this book by reviewing some of the key points of how not to lose. This information is so important in determining your success that it cannot be stressed enough.

I asked you to remember some quotes at the beginning of this book.

"The more things change the more we must embrace the things that never change."

As we move along through the different stages of life, our circumstances certainly change. However, as it relates to planning our financial future, some factors leading to success have not, and will not change.

- Clearly defining our goals

- Identifying the return necessary to achieve our goals

- Defining our tolerance for risk

- Developing, implementing and refining a strategic plan for the management of our assets

"The future ain't like it used to be."

This quote from Yogi Berra leaves us asking - What have we learned from our past mistakes that can help us to avoid losing in the future? Should our objective be to "beat the market" at all costs? Hopefully, you have learned two things relating to this statement. First, it is difficult for most professional managers, and virtually all individual investors, to beat the market over extended periods of time. Second, the return of "the market" is irrelevant if you have a clearly defined set of objectives designed to meet your unique financial goals.

"Financial 'unemotional discipline' is learned, not inherited."

"Investment return is far more dependent on investor behavior than on mutual fund or security performance."

We need to understand and accept that the financial markets are:

- Largely Efficient

- Random and Unpredictable

- Volatile and Risky

In order to learn "unemotional discipline" we need to:

- Develop and execute a long-term financial strategy.

- Control our emotions.

- Remain focused.

- Understand the risk inherent in the financial markets.

- Understand that the markets self- correct.

- Understand that the average will play its role as long as you start with the right mix and allow yourself to stay in the game.

"Randomness Favors The Prepared."

This quote by Taleb is one of the most important, relevant and accurate statements I have ever read. As we have discussed, being prepared takes time. Collect all the information you can. The more information you have, the better prepared you will be for the randomness of the financial markets.

Data mining, stress testing, Monte Carlo analysis and re-sampling will help you to control your emotions when dealing with randomness. You will have the education and knowledge of studying history, as well as mathematically modeling your future assumptions. While it's not possible to predict exactly what will occur in the future, you can become better prepared for the random events that cause the financial markets to experience volatility that is outside of the norm. You will reduce your risk of "blowing up" and not have to venture into the "dynamite factory." One thing is assured in trying to achieve your financial goals: **It is critical to "stay in the game."** It is only by staying in the game that you will allow yourself to earn the average returns of the investments you choose, and have any chance of achieving your financial goals. In order to "stay in the game" you must control your emotions.

I will leave you with one last quote from Taleb and his book Fooled by Randomness:

"I am convinced that after spending almost all of my adult and professional years in a fierce fight between my brain (not fooled by randomness) and my emotions (completely fooled by randomness) in which the only success I've had is in going around my emotions rather than rationalize them. To rationalize them is to subject yourself entirely to the luck or randomness of what will happen."

Take the time to change your behavior and do what is necessary to succeed. If this means engaging professionals to assist you, take the time to investigate and choose the right professionals.

Stop cutting corners, ignoring what is important and basing everything on your emotions.

Learn how to win!

Dennis P. Barba, Jr., Ph.D.